Always

and

Forever

Always

and

Forever

Jacquelyn Knight

Always
and
Forever

Cover design by: Forever And A Day Publishing LLC
Interior design by: Waseem Aziz at waseem@arrowupz.com
Edited by: Forever And A Day Publishing LLC
Published by: Forever And A Day Publishing LLC
Triangle, VA www.faadpublishingllc.com
ISBN: 979-8-9988364-5-9

First Edition

Printed in the United States of America

FAAD
FOREVER AND A DAY PUBLISHING, LLC

DEDICATION

Dedicated to my beloved daughter, Kirsten; my son, Harvey; my three grandsons, Harvey, Roman, and Rahmir; my godson, Cameron (HKHRRC); and to my unwaveringly supportive family.

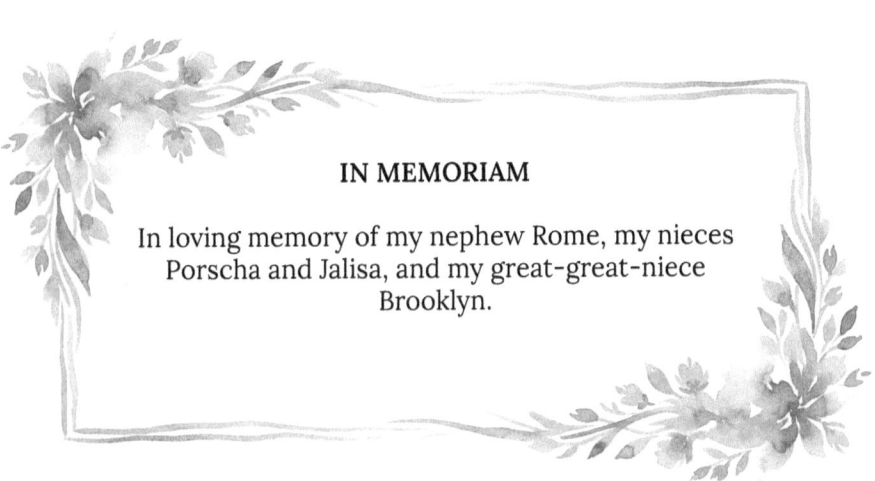

IN MEMORIAM

In loving memory of my nephew Rome, my nieces
Porscha and Jalisa, and my great-great-niece
Brooklyn.

INTRODUCTION

My words are always and forever true, flowing from deep within my heart. The words I long for my sisters and brothers to hear come from a very special place. They are not bound to one spot, but travel everywhere, touching all the issues of life.

When there is doubt, it can feel as if there is no sunshine—only rain and pain. Yet even in those times, God can cover us with a blanket of light. Like a red butterfly whose wings carry strength, my words carry a touch of love that never fades.

I speak always, on the highways and byways, in the daily walk of life. These poems are words of encouragement, given to offer strength and love in everyday situations. They are born from faith, and they find their roots in the Word of God.

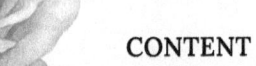

CONTENT

Faith, Patience, and a Miracle

A woman with an illness for some time,
A man not trusting
A life that was saved and seemed like a miracle
Because of love, the time of love
The angel of faith, patience and trust will show up
In time you will have heard, have trusted, and have the
knowledge of
This amazing love.

A special way
That came from tears
How was I going to reach you
No phone call no traveling road
I cried out "Help me, Jesus"
As tears fell from my eyes
I was pulled down on my knees
And began to talk to an angel
And listed to my hearts desires to reach you
That you were embraced with peace, joy, and love today
For the angels arm reaches everyone

Good morning to a thankful and blessed day.

Let us open our eyes to this beautiful day and see God's beautiful creations.

As we can see the beautiful butterfly bouncing around.

We should open our eyes to their beautiful colors.

God has given them the strength to fly around as He gives us the strength to fly around life's overwhelming situations that we may have sometimes in our lives.

We have been given encouragement, hope, simplicity, trust, wisdom, and peace.

Like the butterfly has wings to fly with, God has given us His words and His Love to have faith to make us.

Let's keep His words of understanding and His unconditional love flying around us throughout the day.

We are,

    we are truly,

        truly blessed today.

We are,

    1 might say like the beautiful yellow butterfly

        flying around and around the beautiful

            sunshine, giving off the warmth of

                love.

The beautiful sky with all the beautiful white clouds and the
beautiful red bird flying so freely.

Let me think about this moment.

We are free

    and we are safe,

        also because of the blood of our

            precious Jesus, our family.

    All love and peace among us; especially God's love.

Memories of a Good Day

Thinking of the **Good** times
Thinking of the **Good** food
Thinking about the **Good** weather
Thinking of how **Good** you looked
Hair and clothes
Thinking about how you felt
The love and compassion
Every **Good** gift and every perfect gift is from heaven
A gift called memory
A gift that everyone has received
When you are alone with Jesus and you begin to smile
And think back to **Good** times that you share
With a loved one or met a stranger that day
But the best memory
Is to have the one that is in your heart that is loved

If you can see a beautiful blue sky
If you can see the beautiful sun
If you can hear the birds singing
If you can feel the warmth of that beautiful sunshine
If you can feel the warmth from the wind
Embrace the quietness of the moment
When you can give thanks to God for the start of the beautiful
day

Forgiveness is something that we come in contact with because we are not perfect.

We have to give forgiveness because we have to ask for forgiveness too. Because you are my Sister and Brother, I will forgive you as you will forgive me. If you think I am not thinking about you, please forgive me.

I am always thinking about you through that special act called Prayer.

Good morning to a blessed and beautiful day that God has blessed us to be partakers.

How can we prepare for the wrong and the overwhelming issues of life, or should we?

Sometimes, we just need to Give Love, Be Love, Show Love, Stand on Love.

We need to have a talk with someone who does not reply back, "If I were you, I wouldn't take that mess."

For there is a friend named Jesus who will listen because of our Father God.

The wrong can be made right for He will maintain the Cause.

So stand in His strength, His amazing love for us.

For all the tears that fall from our eyes.

He will wipe them away with Love.

This is your Easter Basket

A: Can *arise because* of Jesus taking all of my cares to Him, especially the one I do not understand and the one that troubles me. They can be so close and then so far away.

P: *Praying* for deliverance from all sins, knowing and unknowing. and asking for forgiveness.

R: For I can be *restored.*

I: I am precious and beautiful in His eyesight.

L: Everlasting **LOVE**, unconditional **LOVE**, a **LOVE** that holds my hands. A **LOVE** that guides my feet. A **LOVE** that I can feel and see day by day. A **LOVE** that is there for me when I need to cry and laugh and when I need comfort in life's issues.

Do you know of Me?
Do you see Me?
Do you hear Me?
Do you feel My presence?

I have words for you about My love for you, these words are in the Bible for you. And when you have tears of joy, clapping hands, moving feet, praises of thanks, I am in your presence.

I am always speaking to you from my angels.
Speaking to you, from me, speaking some amazing things.
Remember My angel 'Gabriel.'

If you ever feel overwhelmed or full of a sweet, so sweet feeling, know that it is also My presence being with you. When you feel like or think that I am far away, I am not.

Or when you need your loved one, a brother or a sister near you and they seem far away, there is a long distance call for you to reach them called *Jesus*.

Sometimes self is unsure
Sometimes self is happy
Sometimes self is sad
Sometimes self is smiling
Sometimes self is crying
Sometimes self is full
Sometimes self is empty
Sometimes self is lost
Sometimes self is overwhelmed
Sometimes self is running, but never finish the race.

For self only need to have running friends
That whisper "Don't give up!"
I am with you right now so let self go
And reach for my hand and hold on
I will also guide your precious feet
To win that trophy
Of self-PEACE and self-PATIENCE and self-LOVE

Out in the GARDEN picking flowers, for it is a GREAT and GOOD day to have GAINED the love to share with others in darkness due to life issues.

To be GRATEFUL of all little things that are surely a blessing that happens to us, and for us, and don't let a negative sign hold us down or bring tears to our eyes that cannot be wiped away with a GREAT hand.

GATHERING together with our loved ones to GIVE thanks and praise to our GOD for His Blanket of Love that keeps us warm when life seems cold. By the GRACIOUS of politeness and forgiveness that we have.

Today.

Today, first of all you may have a smile on your face because of the word 'Thankful'.

Graceful being surrounded by the present of a gift of brightness and a love called Jesus. So unique in size and time that you have a big heart.

That is so amazing! When amazing things happen in and around your presence, you are loved and a blessing today.

Life can be like a season during the year. You might have a plan to do something and it doesn't work out the way you plan so therefore, your plan might seem COLD like the WINTER.

Remember our plans are not God's plans for our life. We find ourselves wondering what to do next. Do we just give up or make another decision about something else?

It's okay because just like a flower begins to grow in the spring time when the temperature changes, we also have to change our attitude to a positive setting.

Moving forward and not backward like the brightness of the sun in the summer time. So warm and bright and the goodness of another blessed day for us to partake in.

Doing something wonderful like smiling, spreading love, being thankful and giving God thanks.

Sometimes it seems like we fall short but remember there are arms of love that can reach us and pick us up.

So no matter what season it may seem like we are going into, as day-to-day life issues bring about.

Just remember the women with the issue of blood. Because of her faith she did not give up. That faith is for you and me also.

In that place so easy to find ourselves
if yesterday seems to be filled with troubles of the
world.
I am first, I am blessed, better and beautiful. I say beautiful
because I do the best talk and when I talk.

I'm talking with Jesus and I do the best walk because I'm
walking by faith and that I can do when those troubled times
come about.

Me and my loved ones, my friends, and all God's
children for sometimes we have to hold each other's hand
when we don't understand.

 Trying to find that perfect moment is somewhat and
sometimes hard. Our HEARTS are overwhelmed with sadness
for a moment, but because we are BLESSED and BETTER and
BEAUTIFUL, we can talk and walk
with
PEACE-LOVE-JOY for today.

For the angels told me to
TRUST IN GOD
and to
TRUST GOD.

Just eyes and beautiful eyes,
Looking from behind the beautiful sun shining so bright.

Eyes that can see the brightness in life, overwhelming issues
or unexpected issues are those extra moments that run on and
on.
Like Noah, that walk with Jesus, he was a just man.

Those just eyes or with Jesus also
That beautiful rainbow that comes when...that beautiful sun
shine
No talking, just walking and smiling and looking out of those
beautiful eyes.

I am like a flower today
for today is my day to blossom
beginning with the rising of the sunshine I am
going to grow to stand tall and firm
because of my rich, oh so rich soil or should
I say my foundation, my foundation today
is Jesus
because I know if I keep my foundation the same
the same because of life issues
I can always stand tall and do not fall
to the circumstances for I grow and most of
all my faith has grown into a blessed
and beautiful sight
where I have
blossomed into a beautiful flower
that is planted in a pot of rich soil
that is rich in **Love**
and strength for today

A beautiful green plant never changes because the soil that the
root sits in is so rich
and
the pot that holds the plant
and
soil is so strong, it gives the plant the strength to grow.

Our faith in God is because of our rich soil
and
strong pot.

We can be strong and stay beautiful because our pot, in life's
circumstance, is Jesus. There are showers of blessings that
include the brightness of light that comes from the beautiful
sunlight.

I wonder where that beautiful Red Bird goes when the day is filled with rain and wind?
Because he is one of God's Creations.

God also keeps him from hurt and danger.
"Let no weapon form."

We are all God's beautiful children and He keeps us from hurt and danger on those days that we know nothing about.

That is what will happen.
As for that beautiful Red Bird, I don't know if there is a weather forecast for him to go by like, "Man, there is a weather forecast for us about the rain and wind."

But the one thing that the bird and man share, there is no weather forecast needed.

For the time when the rain and wind come on those days, the one thing that the bird and man have in common is an umbrella. An umbrella named Jesus.

God has given us Jesus on those days to keep us from the rain that may fall and the wind that blows issues in our lives.
Just believe and know you are loved and beautiful today.

Always and Forever
My days were filled
with so many lessons—
whenever an issue arose,
there always seemed to be an Angel
with amazing words,
words that gently brightened the moment,
or perhaps made the trouble fade away,
not so far that I forgot,
but far enough for me to smile again.

Like beautiful sunshine,
a yellow butterfly drifted
among yellow roses,
and I felt the warmth of that light,
the arms of my Angel embracing me,
keeping me from falling
to the struggles of life.

Instead, I stood tall,
like the beautiful trees.
To be embraced with compassion,
to be embraced with encouragement—
"always" and "forever"
are the words that walk with love.

Because there is an Angel
who will always and forever love you,
and love me,
for our roses may be different colors,
yet all are beautiful.

Good morning,

Because we were standing on the
foundation of love, JESUS,

We were amazed by the rocks
and the stones that came toward us
but never touch us or hurt us

Why, because we were standing
on that foundation of love,

Jesus

Always and forever.
And when I think again,
my heart is filled
with an overflowing, peaceful place
that sometimes overwhelms me—
in the best way—
and makes me smile for you and me.

Because there is a word called love,
and sometimes love needs other words
to help us move through our struggles.

For today,
Love is I and You.

Jacquelyn Knight

About the Author

Jacquelyn Knight is a published poetry author, storyteller, and creative voice who resides in Atmore, Alabama. She is a dedicated mother, grandmother, and godmother, and enjoys spending time going to church, reading the bible, traveling, writing, and being in a positive and peaceful place.

With a passion for being a present-help to all who know her, Jacquelyn uses storytelling to encourage people to change their mindset into a positive one. She inspires all to be open to something or someone new because you never know, a stranger may be an angel. Her journey as a writer began during marriage and she realized that as she was self-comforting, through positive thoughts, to make it through difficult times. She committed to be positive when removing bad thoughts and experiences and over time, writing became a way to share wisdom and encourage positivity.

This book was curated through social media posts and through feedback from others. She was led to take those posts and publish the writings into this published book. This book of poems and thoughts reflect Jacquelyn's belief that God can and will heal. She believes that even though your day may begin a little rough, you can change the ending by changing your thoughts.

As an author, Knight strives to reach readers who need encouragement, offering work that is uplifting, relatable, and faith-filled. Her prayer is that this book provides words that hug you when you need a friend while embracing the journey of growth, purpose, and creativity.

Philippians 4:13 (KJV) I can do all things through Christ which strengtheneth me.

www.ingramcontent.com/pod-product-compliance
Lightning Source LLC
Chambersburg PA
CBHW020321150626

46552CB00022B/3125